Snoballs for All

Snoballs for All

Alexander Brian McConduit
Illustrated by Paulina Ganucheau

PELICAN PUBLISHING COMPANY

CRETNA 2015

To Sage, for bringing me light when there was only darkness.
I love you.—A. B. M.

To Roy and Ruby —P. G.

The word "Pelican" and the depiction of a pelican are
trademarks of Pelican Publishing Company, Inc.,
and are registered in the U.S. Patent and Trademark Office.

Library of Congress Cataloging-in-Publication Data

McConduit, Alexander Brian.
  Snoballs for all / by Alexander Brian McConduit ; illustrated by
Paulina Ganucheau.
       pages cm
  Summary: When young Paul hears a call, "Snoballs for all," he leaves
school and goes running through the streets of New Orleans seeking
the frozen treat.
  ISBN 978-1-4556-2002-9 (pbk. : alk. paper) — ISBN 978-1-4556-
2003-6 (e-book) [1. Stories in rhyme. 2. Frozen desserts—Fiction. 3.
Festivals—Fiction. 4. New Orleans (La.)—Fiction.] I. Ganucheau,
Paulina, illustrator. II. Title.
  PZ8.3.M45944Sno 2015
  [E]—dc23
                          2014025303

Printed in Malaysia
Published by Pelican Publishing Company, Inc.
1000 Burmaster Street, Gretna, Louisiana 70053

Snoballs for All

Down by the bayou, where the grass grows tall,
in a schoolroom sits a little boy named Paul.
While doing his work, he stands up real tall and says,
"Shh! Do you hear that?"

Snoballs *for all!"*

"Exquisite! Who is it who would call such a call?"
Paul says to himself as he runs through the hall.
Through doors and the floors with rackets and balls,
there it goes again: **Snoballs** *for all!*

Paul bursts through the doors and looks at the sky.
It was such a hot day with the sun up so high.
As he stands in the heat and lets the sweat fall,
Paul says, "I have to find where there are **snoballs** for all!"

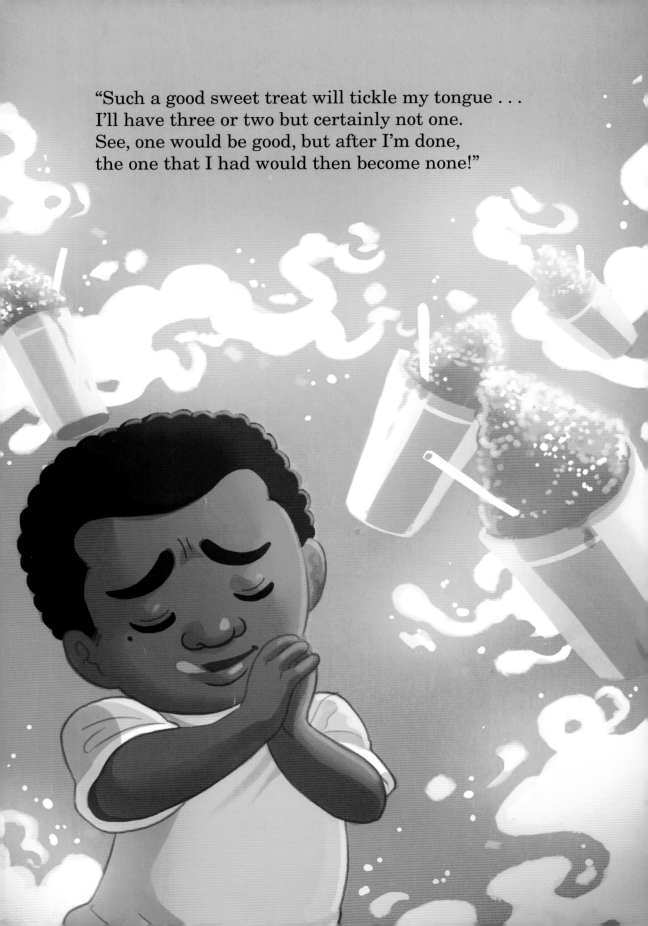

"Such a good sweet treat will tickle my tongue . . .
I'll have three or two but certainly not one.
See, one would be good, but after I'm done,
the one that I had would then become none!"

"So search on, I will, for the call of all calls—
there it goes again . . ."

Snoballs for all!"

"That's it! I quit! Where are you?" Paul screams.

"Where are the **snoballs**,

the **snoballs**

with condensed milk and cream?

"The grapes and strawberry's and wedding
cakes with no top,
with ice cream and gummy bears and sweet,
sweet gum drops."

"The mangos and rainbows of every color in the world.
"Spearmint teeth for us boys and blueberry tongues
for the girls."

"So my search I shall start—on to the park!

Where are the snoballs for all?

I shall look until dark.

When the moon comes out and the sun is asleep,
I should hear clearly 'cause there won't be a peep."

"So wait I shall, until there's a call from somewhere in the distance:

Snoballs *for all!*

"Could it be? Is it me? Or did it come from over there?"

"Near the Superdome? Or City Hall by the mayor?"
So on Paul goes, all the way there,
on the streetcar past the oak trees and right up the stairs.

"Mr. Mayor," Paul asks, "Did you call out the call?"
"What call?"
"You know, **Snuballs** *for all!*"

"I did not."
"Well then, who?"
"I don't know. Was it you?"
"It was not. So I see:
it looks like **snoballs** for all
but no **snoballs** for me!"

How dare they scream Snoballs for all
and not even have one Snoball for Paul?

"It's unfair!" he screams, "Unfair indeed,
to have so many snoballs when there's only one I need."

On he goes with his search. "I must find the call,
the call that screams out, Snoballs for all!"

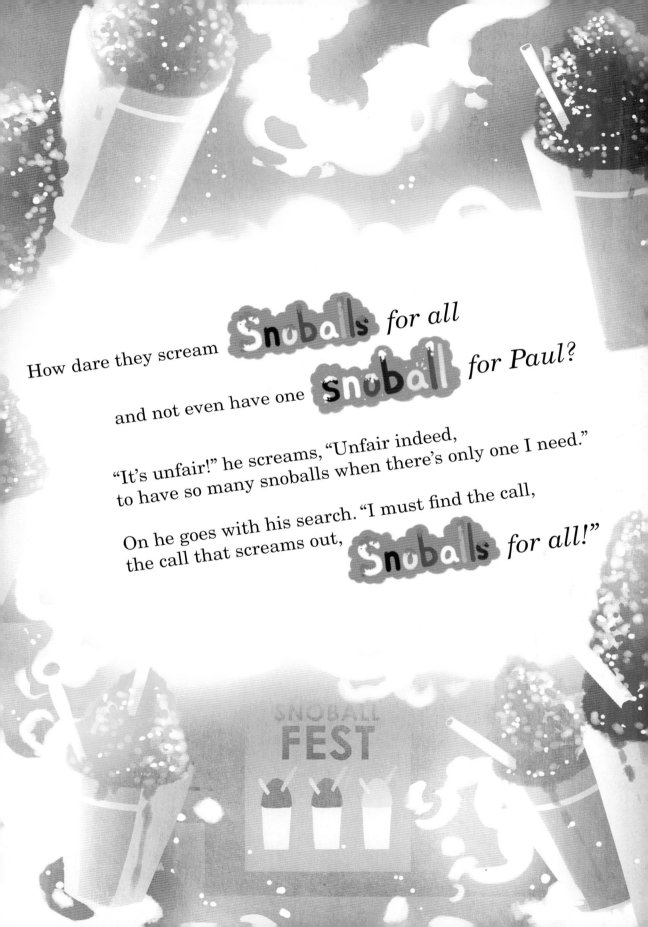

"That's it! I know! I know where they are,

those **Snoballs** for all, let me hop in the car.

"I'll drive on down to the **Snoball** Fest

and finally put the search for **Snoballs** to rest."

As Paul gets to the gates, he hears it real loud,
jumps out of the car, and pushes through the crowd.

"So close—I can taste that delicious, frozen ball,
shaved ice with syrup that I dare not let fall."

"Now that I'm here, I think I want them all!"
And louder than before echoes

Snoballs *for all!*

Over Paul's shoulder is the most beautiful sight:

snoballs to his left

and **snoballs** to his right,

fudge, pralines, and king cakes too.
He will wait no more—he must
now order two:

"I'll have cherry on one; the other, apricot pear!
Triple-extra-large please, and the price, I don't care."

"I've waited long enough and no more do I dare.
One bite, and paradise! I'm on my way there."

"So here I go! Goodbye! It is now time to eat

the  snoballs for all,

and

all snoballs *for me!*"